The Number Six

Jack Beers

These six bees are insects.

These six beetles are insects.

These six flies are insects.

These six dragonflies are insects.

These six wasps are insects.

These six grasshoppers are insects.

All insects have six legs!